Efflorescence

A Feminist Poetry Collection

Zoe Spoor

NEW DEGREE PRESS

COPYRIGHT © 2021 ZOE SPOOR

EFFLORESCENCE

A Feminist Poetry Collection

ISBN

978-1-63676-800-7   *Paperback*
978-1-63730-242-2   *Kindle Ebook*
978-1-63730-243-9   *Digital Ebook*

To my mom and her beautiful soul.
Thank you for the endless support;
I love you to the moon and back.

Contents

Author's Note

Dear Readers,

As a young woman, I've experienced, seen, and heard many accounts of gender inequality and bias, whether that be directed towards myself or other women. I've also endured my own experiences of sexual assault, ones that left me feeling dirty and violated, as well as hearing many of my female friends struggling from this issue. It's striking, when talking to women about such matters that almost every single one, no matter where identities intersect, has experienced gender bias or sexual harassment. With the birth of the fourth wave of feminism, social media has become a new outlet and brought light to copious new injustices, specifically the #MeToo movement. Many college-aged women have experienced sexual assault, and those closest to me, as survivors, made me explore more about what it means to be a feminist. I therefore decided to delve deeper into the subject, as I wanted to create poems that highlight those disparities and represent these realities in forms of new fashion, in a way that can be both beautiful and devastating at the same time.

In high school, I first began using art as an outlet to create works that explore the nature of feminism. In college, I started writing poetry on the side to fill in the gaps where art could not speak. My passion progressed as my world became bigger. I realized the harsh realities of what it means to be a woman, and going through college, I started to become immune to the way I was being treated. A sense of normality set in, serving to the solitude that this happens to everyone, and undermining the caustic consequences it can have. As many women do, I became content with the way we are sexualized, and the way gender roles have shaped the minds of boys and girls. But soon my eyes were opened through various accounts of gender role strains and stories shared by female peers. I wanted to find a way to speak to these injustices. Through poetry, I strive to tell the stories of every woman, and to show their power and progression through time. I believe poems can be expressed with intense emotionality, to convey not only the vulnerability of a woman but also represent us in a way that makes each incredibly strong.

As I conducted more research through interviews and books, I developed the viewpoint of what many think of as a "typical feminist." It was that of a radical individual, one who believes in the superiority of females, or "man haters," which, of course, is not the case. I therefore wanted my book to be about the true ideology of feminism—that we strive for equality of both genders, and that gender roles uniformly hurt both men and women. To do so, I realized I must aim to create a new world within each page, poems that convey the fight for justice and bring realization to such inequalities. I want my book to bring forth everyday life from the woman's perspective, such as falling in love, becoming a mother, or growing up as a teenage girl. These seemingly mundane matters bring the poetry alive within the pages, giving power, depth, and plasticity to each story.

I was called to create a book that would educate others and expand perspectives. I've been interested in feminism for a long time, and, as I became older, I saw a historical absence in the representation of women of color and trans women. I felt a call to action to write an inclusive book, expressing inequalities faced by all, not just heterosexual cis-gendered women, whom feminism was originally intended for. There is also intense discrimination when intersectionality comes into play, which is not discussed enough in the mainstream media.

As a first-time author, I wanted to take on this broad idea in a way that honors each part of the spectrum. That these biases impact everyone—not just the ones women face but also those men face—which highlights that there is no freedom from repression until we are all equal.

I want to share this intimacy through poetry, interlinking each line to create music through words. This book will appeal to fans of poetry, feminists, and the new age of readers—young millennials and Gen Z. Although the scope of this book is broad, it is also ideal for any reader interested in becoming educated on matters that are often difficult to discuss.

My poetry features inclusive stories from women—some from my own experiences, and others from individuals in my own life, or research. It will spotlight the day-to-day struggles and strengths of empowerment. I intend to connect each in the modern fight for equality, and what it truly means to be a feminist.

With sincerity,
Zoe Spoor

Introduction

"I am not free while any woman is unfree, even when her shackles are very different from my own."

— AUDRE LORDE

Efflorescence

Noun

ef·flo·res·cence | eh-fleur-es-since

1:

    a: The birth or flowering of a newly vibrant bloom
    b: Start of blooming or sprouting
    c: Flowering, synonymous with opening

2:

    a :Manifestation of internal vibration to culminate a
    fullness of soul

Abelia, Flora, Wisteria
With bright consummate blooms
Their robust petals sweet,
Below cherry tree loom
Hibiscus, Amaryllis, Lily
Awaken chartreuse stems
Transfer vivid fragrancy
Like the light of lucent gems

We manifest these blooms
Into symbols of present hope
And knock away the doom
Of failure we can scope
Before the sunlight hits shadows
Free to bask in all its rays
We must move forth with grit and heart
To see fiery blooms blaze

PART ONE

Affliction

"Women have served all these centuries as looking glasses possessing the magic and delicious power of reflecting the figure of man at twice its natural size."

— VIRGINIA WOOLF, *A ROOM OF ONE'S OWN*

"Boy"

The skin bites at former flesh
Flesh that grows
A 5 o'clock shadow
And time won't stop
For me to plead to my skin
That it has something else to give

Father forgive me I'm killing your son
Who's wrapped up inside
The bones of someone
Born with a brand
To be a man forever
Although with your accepting hand,
Father, my heart might turn tender

I want to dance under moonlight's kiss
As it reflects off golden hair
And black cherry lipstick
Lets my healing heart dare

But my skin crawls with the thought
Of losing your trust
By a loneliness brought
To my skin's surface

Plastic

Your heart is made of plastic
You mold it to fit me
You mold it to fit other girls,
Late at night to see

You say I'm the only one
Getting special treatment
As you lay your kisses on my mouth
You fill my head with secrets

The hope you fabricate
Gives me pain to spill in trust
Barriers between our hearts break
I question if your love is only lust

Your soul's in my throat
And it's there for you to eat
I spill all of my secrets
Down onto your feet

You wipe them off your shoe
And they lie upon the ground
Like plastic pollution in the sea
Dumb girls who stick around

There are plenty of adhesive hearts
From other fragile souls
Girls you stepped on with dirty shoes
Hoping they don't stick to your soles

Oil Eyes

Your gaslighting sears my heart
Like fried steak and blackened onions
I choose not to make a scene
Because the flies that drip from your mouth
Convince me that your shouting
Is validated
That I'm wrong
Wrong
Wrong

Thick oil eyes fill with rage
Twisted as black fills your sockets
Glassy pupils cut from your soul
You're screaming at me, it's my fault
That we always fight
Buzzing fills me until your voice
Is the only thing I hear
And as you lean in near you whisper
Into my ear: "If you really loved me
You wouldn't act this way"
And I do love you
Which is why I can't leave
Your oil eyes

Stained Skin

Your lopsided smile radiated
Dull winter rooms
Even needle marks stained
Pale skin like cherries

A silence of your presence
At my proudest moments
No hug at graduation,
No teary eyed wide smile
When I started college,
No side of a moment to share

I missed a world others taste
Replaced with sour absence
The world is a dam that distracts
The raging river of my mind
The water always metallic
When it hits the back of my throat

But mom held me close
Tender wrapped in a blanket of arms
Like an iron shield, its impenetrable force
Hidden from lion eyes
Prowling on my heart,
My trust, my innocence

Mom stood strong for her baby girl
Whispered sunsets in her ears
One parent replaced two
In a world of raging rivers

Waterfalls

The tense yarn
Between our hearts
Won't be cut
By kisses, poems, art

Jumping off waterfalls
To distract from the bitter truth
That your heart belongs to
Another girl from your youth

So in the car we sit
Eyes motionless in the sun
Fingers on my lips
To stop from screaming
That you were never mine to begin with

Heart of Holes

The woes you speak to her
Trouble my restless mind
I toss and turn to moonlight's kiss
As bedsheets swallow bitter truths and lies

When you confide in her
It perforates ugly words through
My heart with battle scars
Leaving scarlet lacerations
These thoughts like salt,
Shriveling my tired body
Until there is no water left in me,
Only thick blood and murky veins

Your deafening madness
Does not reach my ears
Because she tastes sweeter than me
Like rhubarb pie on a dewy spring day
She coats your teeth with sugar lies
And cloaks of bright sunshine flowers

I tell myself it's not cheating
If your fingers don't graze her thighs
Or if your mouths refuse to mingle
But I know your heart is hers to keep

As he assembles her fragmented soul
Mine seeps into the sodden earth
And mud eats away my heart with holes
Until I forget it ever existed

Butterfly Wings

Most of the time
Her heart turns black
A hole where memories fade
But sometimes they flood back
Breaking the dam, letting waves
Flash-flood images of him
Taking his time with her body
And she would do anything to forget
His skin coarse like tree bark and
His chubby hands sticky as sap
That wrapped around her neck
Like the paper-thin morbidity
Of butterfly wings

Divinity

Divine like an angle
A feverish essence of bliss
To the people she touched
A vivacious soul
With an untamed heart
Letting it see the world
But not fully basking in its light
For fear of pleasure
Erotic and carnal
Scared to build the bridge of trust
Because the last time
She gave her heart away
Someone took her divinity

Limerence

Comfort from a sweet bottle of acrid liquor
Burning through the memories
Into oblivion, pain bleeds away
My soul is occupied by stars
From the poison filling my head
Where my body is supposed to lay
In a lump of molasses haze
Until the stars burst
And reality brings back
The sting I can't seem
To drink away

The Box

There once was a girl
Who fought for herself
Her wounds opened
When she wondered
What her father might think

Scars left stories of the past
When reminded of what she was
And what she was not

Father wanted a boy
A barrel-chested man
But rather
God gave him what he didn't ask for

So her fragility turned to scars
Thinking she was only worth wounds
But as she grew older, and prouder, and brave
She realized these scars were not ugly;
They were their own kind of bloom,
Reminding her of own her beauty
Inside her heart of efflorescence

So she locked it in a box
And threw away the key
But sometimes, just sometimes
She would open that box
And let the world see

Her fearless eyes focused
Her upturned lips undaunted
She made the world her own
Showing her father a valiant heart
He could not ignore
And slowly his defiant grit gave way
To a melted heart
He knew he couldn't keep away

Feathers

Women on barren sand beaches
Where there's nothing and no one to
Speak up to for rights and pain
But the delicate feathers that cover the beach
In rain or shine transpire to teach
The misgivings of the repressed
Because of how they talk, act, dress

They've had enough
To take a leap of faith
And to not sleep on reformations
Of actions history taught

Yet sometimes the reach is too far
Our arms outstretched and our faces strain
Because it pains us to think
That we cannot do better
And it all started from searching
For delicate feathers

Virgin

Bathed in virtue
Idealized from a faith
That has kept us silent
Sewn our lips closed
And glazed over our eyes
Pearled like a calm ocean floor
Vestal virginity
Consecrated to chastity
Glorified for an obligation
Because women must be
Pure
Innocent
Unable to explore the world
Because the fear
Of slander and disgrace

Glass Cuts

A poet doesn't kiss and tell
But she can taste intentions on your tongue
The pieces of her windowless heart
Are easy to sweep up
They will slice your fingers
As warm blood filters out
Bitter melancholy dreams
That will wake you up
With sweat-soaked sheets

Almost Mine

I want your heart to be mine
I want to open it and climb
Into your chest
But your love is there
It's there to rest

Cold Beds

You're so in love with yourself
That love only happens
In hotel rooms,
But loneliness will
Seal your eyes
And clot your heart
With black blood, and yet
The world will keep rotating
Around the sun even if
Your hear ceases to beat

I hope you enjoy
Your own company
But empty bedsheets feel different
When no one is thinking of you

PART TWO

Justice

"We've begun to raise daughters more like sons. . .but few have the courage to raise our sons more like our daughters."

— GLORIA STEINEM

Fruitful

Is there a film in existence
Which doesn't hurt young minds
Condition them to think
The genders aren't intertwined

Objectification in movies, ads, books
Only hurts us,
The rain that waters our roots
Nourishes rotten weeds
Strangling the ivy growing up our trees

Stealing our precious water
Will ensure our blooms don't flower
We must wake up from this fever dream
And see reality of the media's mainstream

It lies and spies and preys upon
Our unsound hearts getting hurt so fast
Be careful or you'll become the victim
The weeds will not be the last
To suck our water away
So fortify your roots with thorns and
Down in the valley let your branches sway

Boys Can Cry

I shuddered when I asked him
When was the last time you cried
His answer was not forgotten
His dark face drew in a sigh

"I honestly can't remember,"
He spoke with wicker words,
The battle of masculinity
Makes sure the lines aren't blurred

But I want you to know
It's okay for boys to cry
It's a healthy way to cope
To suppress them is a lie

As you let these sentiments go
And watch them sway in the breeze
To fully express yourself
And set your mind at ease

Expectations surround us
About what a true man is meant to be,
But when will society wake up
And set our boys free

These "precondition men"
Who never feel enough
Because they can't fix the house
Because they don't drive a truck

I am calling you to action
To teach your boys to cry
To uncap that bottle and
Release the pain inside

History has created
An identity of what we are not
It's a template of our entity
The courage to ignore it remains lost

This is why it's crucial
For our teachings to be true
To regulate, not oppress
Is what society should pursue

Womanism

The solitude black women face
Constantly mistreated, outpaced
In every social movement, alienated
Without reform to embrace

Casual sexism ingrained in every blade of grass
And every brick in every building
Feminism is jade, kelly, aquamarine
But for black women it's just green

To refrain from being isolated
Of history's gory past
They form alliances to testify
To fight the unfair social caste

Wearing petticoats lined with mud
Pain plastered on their faces
Raising painted signs higher
Leaving mucky footprint traces

They marched every morning
Into the hot and fleshy ground
They spoke to synthesize union
A voice a balance renowned

To turn history into harmony
They called themselves womanists
And their will to change conformity
Will fuck up white supremacists

Giving Tree

Do you believe in intersectionality?
How the overlapping systems of identity
Create a unique model of discrimination
Like throwing paper into a fire
And watching it shrivel
Into a glow of sapphire

You call yourself a feminist
But you're blind to so much more
Race, class, gender, religion
It's not about which one you stand for

It's a human rights movement
In the nature of being
We are all interconnected
The roots of our giving tree conceiving
While laced in intimacy
Rich in culture, dreams, love, hate
Births a new open field to create

All women means black and trans women, too
Sealing our future is not an easy task
So I ask of you
To acknowledge these differences
To be the one to see
The importance of watering
The roots of our giving tree

Finding Her

When her voice turns blue
And her fingers become ice
The frigid night air
Covers the last slice of green
As hope turns to despair

Snow turns words
Into white whispers
Her sweet voice can no longer be heard
Just the stillness of pine trees
As amber fall transfers

Out she looks from
Foggy windows at night
Thinking seasons will change
As winter lays its blanket of white

But as the snow melts
To the demure spring
Sapping trees reappear
Transcendence of new growth
Hold strong as blooms near

Like pine in icy wind
Unabashed by the masses
She yells to the tree tops
Through the mountain it passes

Through the valleys it rode
Taken in by the wind
She finds herself,
Her voice from within

Past Life

She nods to the past
With a withering heart
Reminiscing
On the meek-mannered girl
Whose jaded eyes
Refused to meet her gaze

She stood before that girl
With valiant eyes
And a bold heart
She said "don't be afraid"
Of what lies in the dark

That her strong-willed soul
Will empower her
And that she will become
The woman
She's always searched for

Bodybags

Oppression doesn't just hurt the oppressed
It also harms those who seem to have it best
He snuffs out a final cigarette
Holds in the smoky drag
Then stuffs his tattered legs
And his soul into a bodybag

Its complex flavors mingle in his mouth
Like biscuits and gravy his mama made down South
The killing tastes so good, why can't we stop?
Because it's easy for an alpha male to stay on top

But he must also fit the constraints
Narrow-minded, old-fashioned forms
Because a "real" man can't complain
Of unfair gender norms

Showing vulnerability, empathy, sadness
To a society filled with conviction
Is complete and utter madness
Yet we think men aren't afflicted

Demasculinized as quick
As lightning hits an open field
Trapped in a constant state of spinning
Like spokes on a wheel

Bloody Rain

Caustic drops of rain
Upon her doleful face
She sticks out her tongue
Just to taste
The metal bite
Like the shackles
That bind cocoa wrists
With every protest
She remains indignant

Electric charge
From the black women by her side
Shoulder to shoulder
A shield for each other
Womanists together
Rich with culture
In the solidarity of race

The white patriarchy surrenders
Until its skeleton's show
As their voices bend its will
And begs to be held
By the arms of umber women
Once the reality of racism
Crawls it bloody way to the light

They will not hold you
Or let your tears fall
Upon strong shoulders
Just to give you peace of mind
To tell you it's okay

It's not

Male Privilege

The reality we face
Is a constant nagging itch
It doesn't go away
Whether wealthy, poor or rich

It festers in our wounds
Infecting and consuming
Feeding on the underprivileged
Overhead, as it looms

I know it's hard to hear
Women beg you to listen
If you open your ears,
Your soul will surely glisten

You don't get interrupted
Or spoken over when you speak
You can sleep with lots of people
And will not face harsh critique

Every large religion
Is run by a man
You can choose to not bear children
Without feeling less than

If you're having a bad day
And in a terrible mood
You will not be blamed
On hormones that are skewed

These just scratch the surface
Of the stereotypes we face
I applaud you for listening
Now our goal: you must chase

Stand with us and for us
All religion, status and race
As an ally for equality
Reform you can help embrace

Why

I love being a woman, but
My gender elicits questions
I'm asked why I'm childless
Then given unprovoked suggestions

My answer remains static, no matter
How crazy I sound, I know my bare skin
Will always remain watered
From my own heart within

I'm not lonely by choice
Because I refuse to bear a child,
And you don't have the right
To comment or revile

I hear utterances you say in shadows,
Don't think they're unknown, but control
What you say, stay mindful of words
That eat away my soul

We do not feel lonely
And we do not cry
It's the "why" that you asked
That makes most of us comply

Rest assured you were not put
On earth to be a womb
That is not the fate
To which you are doomed

Your choice is a virtue
With no morality involved,
The righteousness is your own
Let their judgement be absolved

Pink Tax

Cradled in the jaws of revenue
Living in black and white,
Femininity marked as a necessity,
Products that resemble how we are viewed
And what we should use
As to not confuse the young from an early age
We're conditioned from the air in our lungs
To the blood in our veins that we are owned by
The market and defined by the tears we cry
Pent up, our minds inside know it's wrong
But still we surrender to the marginal profit
Conditioned to think we need
Makeup, waxing, diets and everything in between
Those widened cracks feed
The desperate money monsters
Who make their pink products higher
The cost of being a female consumer
Is no rumor or myth, it's true
We must tell the market there is
No different between pink and blue

1918

Who am I?

I'm a woman with no voice to speak
Identity maligned continuously
Until I harnessed the power of my gender
And cut my string of anguish
I'm yearning for more and
Screaming for activism
To speak my truth

As a woman, I ask
Why is it debauchery
To have influence?
Why is it evil
To possess power of choice?
Seared in their conscious,
I've given way to a reprobate mind

Why can't I vote?

Home of the Free

He said
What more could you want
Our government is great
It's the "best country in the world"
From the sinners to the saints
From the freedom our flag gives us,
To the war troops march towards
America is perfect
In *"every way"* he roared

Firstly,
This land was never ours
I know that to be true
Our daughters, sisters, wives
Don't thrive the way men do

We struggle
To find our own way
Because of past notions
And to America I say
Our system is terribly broken

This perfect country
Has many flaws
From the rights of our bodies
To the maternity leave cause
We fight our own battles
For the rights we cannot choose
The politics are overrun
By white men who refuse
To pass important laws
Protecting victims of rape
Like when oral sex isn't recognized
As assault, will there ever be
A way for women to escape

These seem like dark times
And for that I can say
Hope is not forgotten
Inequalities will be changed
Because there are good people
Who take to office with care
They know past and present struggles
And open arms they come to bare

There will be new horizons
For that I can promise
Because the strength of feminists
Bring omens of new homage

Getting Political

Sexist attitudes pervade politics that
Surround me in a bubble of demise
Prejudice infiltrates them as another white man
Fills the seat, to replace
Yet another white man that came before him

An unspoken conscious fills balmy air as
Hunger gnaws at my throat and
Ambition courses through my veins
These ugly tricks they play
Are not a game I am interested in
"I am just like you"
But my voice carries over snow
Deep enough to get lost
Like a rat in a maze
I am trapped in my own country
Unable to do anything
But hold on to wretched hope
That a new day will bring
New government reform
And a voice for us all

PART III

Dismay

"It's not my responsibility to be beautiful. I'm not alive for that purpose. My existence is not about how desirable you find me."

— WARSAN SHIRE

My Mini Skirt

Does my mini skirt offend you?
Do my naked shoulders invite you
To think I want something?
Does what I wear give you the right
To brutalize my body?
I won't dare let you patronize me anymore
With the strength of the women before me
I take back my sovereignty
The honeyed faces
Of my saccharine children
Will no longer fear misgivings
From people who think
That they own us

Run

Down the sodden pathway
As my legs carry me
My toe digs into gravel
Leaving nothing but debris
I look in each direction
Hoping I'm not being followed
In the desolate mountains
Of small town Colorado

I feel the cold, hard steel
Against the denim of my jeans
Blade at the ready, as
I run past icy streams
Primed to strike its steel
At any given moment,
As I track feet though
Dirt already broken

This knife brings me comfort
When I run on dusty trails
Mother warned me
It's dangerous, yet I can't resist
The wind on my face
And dirt under my nails

Fearful the dense forest
Will swallow me whole
Where I ventured to,
No one will know

I must give up what I want
Because the world is treacherous
Ignorance isn't a blissful jaunt
I must always think again
Before being adventurous

My Favorite Frat House

It all starts harmless, with a sweet little kiss
In the basement of my favorite frat house,
One I will no longer miss.
He reaches for my breasts, and I realize I'm too drunk.
This, I must confess, was my own fault.

I push him away, but he's not easily deterred.
I tell him to stop, but I'm easily ignored.
He grabs my wrists with force,
And up the stairs we climb.
Suddenly I realize I'm running out of time.

Inside his room, walls caving in,
Trapping me inside, I feel his fingers on my skin.
He's holding my arms down as he climbs on top
Paralyzed body, I tell him to stop
Violating me, in my favorite frat house.
I can feel his sweat drip as he holds me down.

My bruised wrists are hurting,
But I cannot make a sound.
Trying to open my mouth,
Yet words refuse to come out.
Disabled by my own fear I can't live without.

When he's finished he leaves, eyes averting mine,
And I cry to myself that I drank too much wine,
But as I grew I realized his actions were malign.

I was not at fault for what happened to me,
And blaming myself
Made my contrite heart unhappy.

The first thing I did was the largest accomplishment.
For the first time in a long time, I felt competent.
I filed a Title IX, the weight of the world lifted off my shoulders.
The feeling of control felt like final closure,

My untold story was ready to unfold.
And I was going all in
Soul dauntless and bold.

But the school had other plans, you see,
Because the man that raped me was a "doctor to be."
He had his whole life ahead of him
One girl couldn't mess it up
So they swept it under the rug, reputations intact.
So my untold story I decided to take back.

Crunchy Curls

People ask to touch
Her crunchy curls, textured and fine
She frowns with
Mahogany skin, deep-set lines
When glassy eyes squint from golden beams
And give way to micro biases

Butter pecan skin
As dark as the night, as golden as the dawn
Beautiful but broken
Sanity barely hanging on

Her scars are invisible to those
With alabaster skin
A blanket covers bones where
Splatter marks paint black skin

As whites wash their hands of
Her skin that seems so strange
They fear her, she's different
Torn down, because static is better than change

Upper class in
The deep heart of Georgia
Surprises the whites when
She drives her Ferrari California

Because she's not supposed to escape
Scars cut deep in the heart
Seldom rise to surface
But her pain always present, always apart

Her skin made of coffee beans
Open doors to discrimination
From systematic institutions
Birthed in home nations

Survivor

Dressed in my Sunday best
The court drenched in sunshine
I feel a weight on my spine
A knock in my throat
The words come out
But they don't feel like mine
I don't own them

He does

He has owned everything
Since that night
My claims dissolving in the air
Turning into frivolous dust
Their ashes on my hands
Afraid the world
Won't believe my words

The court says I'm a victim
I say I'm a survivor

Quid Pro Quo

I can still feel
His hot breath on my neck
Wiry hands groping my breasts
While my mind paralyzed
A helpless body

I was clothed
But I've never felt more naked

He said I'd get promoted
He said I'd get a bonus
He said I'm too beautiful to work in an office
He said I just had to do one thing for him

As his touch slowly slid down
My dress strap
Revealing bare shoulders
And empty eyes

Moonlight Kingdom

As dusk invites light into the sky
You don't answer your phone, and
Mom's worried sick
Dad's in town searching
As the moonlight kingdom fades away
With you still in it

And they worry

You could be face down in a bog
Where driftwood and water lilies
Cover strawberry curls

You could be in a shallow grave
Mingling with mossy dirt
That stains ivory skin
As mold beckons decay

But you're fine
You're with a friend
And your phone's
Just dead

Your brother's out too but
Your parents don't mind
Because the world's full of peril
For someone of your kind

So don't stay out late
In the moonlight kingdom
Where the gleam of stars
Don't seem to shine

1 in 6

1 in 6—
The number of women
Who will be sexually assaulted
In their lifetimes.
Afterward, most are not the same.
Some feel they've lost
Something vital

And they have the audacity to ask
Why it's so hard to come forward?
Fear of embarrassment
Shame
Weakness
Fear they'll say
It didn't happen
And you're lying

If you know more
Than 6 women
You know someone
That has been touched in ways
They did not want

Written and then unwritten again
Because of scrutiny, asked
Were you "too drunk"
Was your outfit "too slutty"
You better hope in the dawned night
Your friends know where you are
Because it can happen to anyone
Protect yourself
From a fickle world
And its unwillingness to change

Needles Under Skin

Swollen magenta peppers my arms
From stringy fingers that grab too tight
I tell him to stop
But he ravishes in the power
His face bathed in the shadows of my soul
I scream silently, but I can't escape
The endless, volatile love and hate
So I ask
How do I stop the pain
Stinging like needles under my skin
Drawing blood and
Offering no bandage after

Strawberry Eyes

She needs her roots to drink
To feed her visceral voice
To speak for girls whose voices are seized
Pallid in the icy night

Hopes of finding a raven's wing
Black as iron oxide left in a barren field of pine
Crisp with wooden musk
Pine needles frosted over blades of grass,
Yellowed from the sun, gasping
For each drop of water
Until there is none left to give life

So she whispers to the pine
"I'm as strong as you in winter"
Windswept and snow stunted,
But survivalists
Tough as nails and strong as silk
Fighting until her petals wilt

The Honor Code

The honor system
Within the cycle of poverty
Had her on a plane to Pakistan
To marry a forty-five-year-old man

She was 15

She got on bruised knees
Purple from playing with the kids outside
Pleaded to her parents
Teary eyed and sobbing
Not to let this man
Rape her every night

But in the cold abyss
Her father showed no emotion
Because she needed to honor her family
So her deep red blood was spilled
Tell me
Where is the honor in that?

She was told to be
A dutiful woman
To listen to her father
And never speak over him
Sometimes her spirit got the best of her
But her mother told her when she married
She would learn
How to be a real woman

She learned to take her clothes off
When he hurt her
Or else he wouldn't stop

She learned to breathe quietly
When anxiety struck her heart
In the blanket of night

She learned to cover her bruises
Where he grabbed too tight
If she ever dared defy him

And she learned to wrap a noose
Around her dainty neck
And how to kick the chair
From underneath her feet

She learned
How to be free from this honor

Catcall

For all women who hear
Unwanted comments by
Sullen strangers
Walk past fast enough
To keep fearful eyes
And shaky hands far away
As to not hear
Their carnal comments

PART IV

Repose

"I hate to hear you talk about all women as if they were fine ladies instead of rational creatures. None of us want to be in calm waters all our lives."

— JANE AUSTEN, *PERSUASION*

Magic of a Woman

Moonlight talks in sunsets
Glazes grassy blades
Traps them in night's solitude
Her heart lay under bodies
As death coats the air with blight
And turns breath thick
Just to feel the burn
Of her loving heart within

When the World Went Blue

She dreams of being a princess
At least that's what she said
She plays with dolls but only because
Those were the only toys
In the box nestled in the corner
Of her pink room

Her birthday party is always pink
Pink cake, pink balloons, pink dress
But nobody asked her if she liked pink
Because nobody thought for a second
To think these stereotypes are archaic

Molded into what they want
Because if her shape
Doesn't fit into the right spot,
The very ground might break in half
And the cracks will scream
As they rip apart
The very earth that turned pink

In One Fell Swoop

We rally and protest,
Ambitions run high
We fight for new rights
Under blue-covered sky
The world's might
Bares dreams unified
Equalize the strata
Of complex humankind

Hills

She bows to the phantom
Barbed-wire fence as
Vast land surrounds
The prison she lives in
Ode to past lives,
As old as hills,
Phantom whispers
She must choose
To live in fear,
Or live in harmony
With equality comes a fight but
As tough as her mother
She will not surrender
To the armored iron cage

Wisteria

Glazed in sunlight
Rays shining from within
A women named Wisteria
Set free all her sins

She bathed in the beams
Glorious and warm
With a sigh of relief
Her being transformed

She let go of the ashes
Black muck blew in the air
The ashes scattered round her
As she surrendered to a prayer

The bad things that she's done
To fight for her own rights
For all the women that hurt
She grieved every night

She prayed for new beginnings
For the world to see her light
A world of equality
In the sky shined bright

The Garden of Congress

The garden was an alluring oasis and she was sure
Her unique motif of clarity
Would be refreshing to the flowers
Dreams of legacy, honor, integrity
Embedded in her mind spoke to the wind

Breeze encouraged her hair to tickle her cheek
The flowers she shared her soul to keep
Her vision like the myth they were but
No one cared
Or thought to listen
To a woman

The wind carried her dreams dauntlessly
As the breeze broke,
It spoke to vibrant trees
In the valley of broken dreams
To let her mold it like warm clay
By her determination

History itself was marked by her
Influence on representation

Gelatinous

Manipulation, intimidation
Frequent corporate education
Muting voices, making them think
They don't mean anything,
Is the key to the lock of patriarchy
Keeping our revelation sour,
Our trepidation sweet
Like a coat of syrup,
Too sugary to eat
Striking nerves when you bite
Into the rich treat
Sticking to teeth
Like cloying molasses walls
Into the hole that swallows us whole
So we release our grasp
To darkness we surrender
We fall

Clementine

My heart burns bright
In fitful moonlight
While the sun withers away

Men's erotic gaze
Turns bodies into toys
My chest is made of oranges
Ripe with attention
Grabbing stares I do not seek

My clementine heart
Bursts with raw bruises
Like peaches and apples
Falling from branches

Fruitful labor to grow
Tumbles on reedy grass
Dents innocuously light
Ruins the perfectly ripe

House of Rep.

You think women belong
Only in the kitchen
To cook up a good meal
For all the representatives to watch
But now we're striking
The house walls
That tried to confine us

Freedom Fire

Away smoke blows like birds in the night
Flying away from danger which withers on sight
The smoke in the air from fire I lit
Coals burning as bright as flames they emit

Carbon is the true carnivore of them all

Thoughts that fill the largest of rooms
Bear weight on the women
Thoughts consume as they
Eat up the air, to action it calls
Because the oxygen is filled
With halls of injustice
Cutting deep as gender strains that are built
Like cinder walls, impossible to burn
Until the ashes of action rise up
Unfair roles to discern

But I lit a fire beneath cement walls
Oxygen eaten up,
Intolerance won't fall
Until you stand with us
Against injustice we face
That's beaten us down
But still we rise, our truths come out
Our speeches carry fierceness that chew through the fog
Speaking rebellion to hearts deep down
We ascend through the fire, a new epilogue

PART V

Passion

"She is free in her wildness, she is a wanderess, a drop of free water. She knows nothing of borders and cares nothing for rules or customs. 'Time' for her isn't something to fight against. Her life flows clean, with passion, like fresh water."

— ROMAN PAYNE

Black Widow

How do I untangle
The fibrous spindles
Carefully threaded between
Spider legs
Without breaking
You in half

Almond Milk Latte

Your skin is
Milk and lavender white waves
Mingling, making coffee dulcet
Sweet like honey
As they mix into a caramel cream
I wish upon a coffee bean dream
That I can once again hear
Your sugary voice
Raspy like a knife glazing toast
But smooth like blueberry jelly
Your sweet talks
And gentle kisses
Are the things I miss
The most

Dew

Hot bodies tangled together
Their fortress of love boundless
Stretching across the universe
Shaping into planets and stars
Forming new pathways
To this heaven

Asteroids of kisses
As fingers trace faces
Closing the space
Between them
Into each other
Until nothing is left
Except two girls
Who chase sunrises
While morning dew
Tickles their feet

When Stars Align

Many things have come and go
But you are a constant
A state of mind
A state of me
I hold onto your saccharine smile
Solicitous and warm
Hope was yours the moment I let go
Your arms safe as a shield
As you wrap around my back
This is where I belong
I finally found my place
Of being

Seashells

Who does she meet
Down by the seashore
Where shells interlace
Foamy water
Mingled with speckled sand
Dusted by sea stars
Where waves fall and rise

Dipping her toes
To unite with the sea
As salty air curls her hair
The beach breathes deeply
To free her saline spirit

Soaring above the clouds
And gliding on waves
Her love stretches, as true blue
As the sea

The sand accepts her
As the wind whistles
To seashells
That in an oblivion of time
She will be buried by the sand

Its grains accept her body
Burying the girl
Who knew self-love
And danced
Among salty horizons

Last Night

Glassy green eyes
Turn to stardust
As your gaze wipes away
Past saline tears
And hands graze upturned cheeks
To remember a night that lasted
An infinity of moments
And stretched to
The moon
The sun
The stars

Tempest Sky

On the tempest days and
The coldest winter nights
I still do not long for your body

Or the touch of your skin
When fingers whispered across my chest
Leaving a trail of warmth

Or waking up to you
Light trickling through the window
Carving out kind eyes and sleepy hair

I do not miss your endless nights
Sharing ecstasy with someone else
Molding your body into hers like you used to with mine

Our love would have moved galaxies if you let it
But all that is left
Are dead leaves on dewy ground

Fallen and forgotten
By the one who let them grow

Drunk Girls & Bathrooms

I look in the bathroom mirror and all I see
Are the things I would change, the flaws that make me
I stare at myself as muffled music blasts
In a club full of people, alone at last
In need of another sugary drink
To forget my big nose, bumpy skin and cheeks too pink

Whether fate or the drinks took action, I cannot say
Because drunk girls in bathrooms came into play
They shower me with compliments and take my hand
Telling me of my crystal eyes and hair like sand

I'm whisked away, although they don't know me,
They do not care because they can see
All that matters is here and now
And how we can dance without spilling Curacao

These women are strangers no more
And I think to myself, how I adore
Drunk girls in bathrooms,
Until dawn hides the moon

Growing Pains

Hoping for a child each night
I give in to the rest
I feel a sense of blight
But won't give up just yet

I keep the pain to myself
I must be careful, I convey
To dream of oneself
To stay fertile, I pray

Then I sense a growing in my heart
Fuller and fuller each day
I did not expect this from the start
A miracle, doctors say

My belly's getting bigger
Growing larger each day
The state of my own vigor
Is where I hope to stay

Finally, the day has come
To hold my child on my chest
And I know my baby
Will set my mind to rest

My Sun

Forever humbled by the blue summer sky
And the cigarette kisses
That always tasted like you
The cherry lip gloss you wore
Artificially sweet in every way
Long blonde hair caressing
Thoughtful eyes made even serenity quiver

People would stare,
Not because we were two girls
With fingers intertwined
And galaxies between gentle love
But because the aura of your beauty
Strikes even the god that created you
He spun you of golden string
And filled you with silken cotton
You are too good for the world
And you are a creation
That is all mine to bare

Enough

Looked at
But not often seen
Talked about
But not listened to
Used, abused, discarded
She hides emotions
Swelling inside her chest
Grounding her to chilled dirt and
Wrapping in spindles of disparity
Like veins constricting the heart
Suffocating the lungs she breathes with

But she could inspire
New prosperity
New beginnings
New thoughts and ideas

If we would just stop to listen
To ponder her thoughts
And stop speaking over women

Tender Heart

My mother always spoke kindly to me
With a voice like warm honey
She would soothe the monsters
Occupying my soul
Like a moon presenting itself
When stars never seemed to align

She caressed my head in golden light
As she'd done a hundred times before
Speaking softly in my ear
She enjoyed being a caregiver
Almost as much as being a mother

She smelled of fresh coffee beans
When she rubbed my silken hair and
Just like worn denim
I could physically see how loved she was
And the sprouting wisdom
She spoke to me
Was her way of letting go
So I could grow into my own identity

Her silken sweater would tickle my cheeks
As I buried my face into her chest
When the world had never seemed to yield
To the growing pains of a teenage girl
My mother gave herself to me
And loved wholly
So that I could love myself

Bare

To wear short skirts and
Feel the wind against her legs
Without fear of judgment
Her inner intelligence
Should be enough to satisfy the world
Where she dances with
Bare shoulders, or tight jeans

Oblivion of a Moment

How can one side of a moment
Be stretched into oblivion
To clip the pages of his face and
Glue them to every facet of her soul and
Fix the cracks where sour wind gales
Hit sails, carrying away his love
Bending the sun and
Ripping the seams of stars
Forever erasing the feel
Of the clouds on his lips and
Soft whispers of breath
Against her neck

Jupiter

Multiple suns in her heart
Beam balletic rays
That push and pull him
In the fabric of space
Fixed as a moment of time
Like bunched bedsheets
Hiding her soul
Before the lunar eclipse
Cast reflective shadows
Back at her fractured soul

Higher Gravity

You love so deeply
It brightens the dark parts of the sea
Light cracks the midnight zone
When your sun rises above
The river of the universe
Pulling to those
Of higher gravity
Pulling you closer to me

Saturn

I want the rings of Saturn
To scoop me into timeless stars
To swallow me whole after sex
Let me smoke cigars
Help me forget

Peach Moons

Peach moons stare down
At shining souls, but
Your soul shines brightest as it
Reaches its dandelion hands
To capture my heart
But my heart can't exist
When your soul
Doesn't want me

PART VI

Beauty

" Those extra five pounds are the best parts of your life. They're dinner with friends, enjoying an extra slice of birthday cake, and drinks you had dancing your ass off at a concert."

— ZOE SPOOR

Granulated

The ravenous predator beneath my skin
Screams for a greedy taste of sugar
I dream of frosted cake and crumbly cookies
While my stomach rumbles to the sleepy shadows
Of my starved mind
My dinner played hooky, I'm dying
To be like the girls in the ads
They don't look hungry
With their slim waist, shapely face
Though the thought of eating consumes my days,
The fear of being ugly is greater than my body
When it screams to be heard

I muffle the shrieks and howls
Because I cannot produce the words
To describe the prowling predators inside

The Dissolving Sun

To embrace sensuality
Is a gift from the heart
Don't wither to the words
Young men can't tell apart

A wilting flower can be watered
And given sunlight to thrive
Slowly its efflorescent blooms
Bring floral lands alive

Like a flower, thorns of willful power
Grow when unified
But be careful darling
The budding of your confidence
Might be misconstrued and
Twisted up like vines

But when courage blooms
Waxen petals will have holes
Gnawed through like garden beetles,
To be sexy and attractive

But not too sexy
Or too attractive

When you let sexuality bloom
The rest will follow suit
Turning a sullen field
In a vibrant oasis of flora
Dawning lucent petals
That drape the stems
Framing them
In a tight dress of red

Flowers will not bloom
Without sunlight

I Can't Win

The curves of my waist
The bulk in my thighs
The plump of my back
Where all the fat lies

To detox I run
Sip on tea and green juice
Shed the bad fat for good
Although to me it seems senseless

It's what makes men want me
What makes most women tick
The way we are viewed
Makes me quite honestly sick

Too fat or too skinny
I really can't win
When I lose the weight fast
The comments begin

"Are you eating enough"
"You look like skin and bones"
"You're too small to be sexy"
"Wouldn't you rather be toned"

But when I love myself
The fat on my tummy
Their words get to me
They make me feel funny

"You won't fit in that"
"Your stomach is showing"
"You must eat like a pig"
"Those pants are overflowing"

I can't be loved in this little space
Small minds are contagious
Where biases are laced
To criticize every action women take

To me it's astounding
How women don't break
When the jaws keep on tightening
Because we pass on the cake

Fluidity

Gender is
An expression
A journey of identity
It can be fluid like
Milk and coffee
Mixing together
Making hazelnut cream

It can be constant
Like the sun as it beams
Unrequited above our heads
How we talk, act, dress
How we are perceived

It's like navigating
Between Scylla and Charybdis
It is the foundation
Of feminism
And if we can comprehend
The fluid nature
Of water before ice

We can unlock new facets
For the human rights movement
Instead of trying to pick
An impossible lock
With only two keys

Belly Rolls

The media has blinded us
Pushed misfortune beyond despair
Minds of our young children with
Beauty standards they cannot bear

But the inevitable has happened
When society tells all
The pressure the youth faces
To the media we must call

To tell them the virtue
Of acne, moles, and rolls
That femininity can be anything
That beauty takes a toll

We can change these norms
And slowly our children will see
Their passion and might
Will be what sets us free

Reflection

I look in the mirror
And all I see
Is a bulging tummy
With curves flowing over
The seams of my jeans
Accentuating flabby arms
And plump cheeks

So I think
I'll finally be happy
When I'm skinny

Right?

Freckles

Splatters of warm taupe
Crinkles around smiling cheeks
In patterns that tell stories of the past
They grow and darken when
Exposed to clement rays
Soft features make way
To let dots speak
Past and present
Distant and distinct
Hazy and crystalline
An unparalleled uniqueness

Some are not yet thought of
Only to be brought about
When paling creases give way
And white strands
Mature to grizzly locks
Varying shapes and sizes
Trying to uniformly fit
Like a game of Tetris

Damaged but beautiful
A sign of age, but seemingly juvenile
A youth, growing and ever changing
To the ways of the world

Tom Boy

I haven't shaved in days
But my boyfriend doesn't mind
He says
All hair is beautiful
In its unique own way

That all hair, everywhere
Sings stories on our body
So my body
Is where my hair will stay

My Youth

My wild body harnesses
Clouds to chase away monsters
As jasmine fills the summer air
And mom hangs fresh linen sheets to dry

With youth comes calm oceans
Like the ones you used to visit
When boyish arms couldn't carry
The weight of school textbooks

We are empowered to let the night sky talk
To drink and smoke and laugh
The beauty of the world is like
A whisper of sweet nothings
With skin so close you can feel the warmth
Blanketing your body
Loving and touching and wanting
Under the burgundy crepe myrtle
Pure and blissful and unrestrained

The eye of the beholder is you
And you're the sunrise wrapped
In a cloak of sunsets

Acknowledgments

I want to express gratitude to those who have helped make *Efflorescence* what it is today. Fulfilling this dream would not have been possible without you. Setting out on this long journey has been such a rewarding experience, and as I poured my heart out to the world, I never realized the amazing people it would bring me. Publishing a book is one of the most difficult things I've ever done, and I discovered along the way that writing and publishing *Efflorescence* takes a village of people. I am so grateful for all of the support.

I'd like to acknowledge those who gave this book a chance and those brave enough to share their stories with me. Thank you for your trust.

Thank you first and foremost to my mom, Grace Babcock, and Joanna Jin for supporting me through every step of the way as well as to my editors Anne Kelley and Emily Price, the Creator Institute, and Eric Koester.

I'd also like to gratefully acknowledge:

Zeta Delta	Ciara Fernandez
Eden Toporek	Jess Vaudo
Shelby Sabourin	Taylor Niziak

Diane Sepkowski

Chloe Jones

Lydia Barnard

Jose Rosario

Koreena Krouth

Olivia Morgan

Emma Claire Glassie

Pia Sharma

Hannah Foster

Heather Layton

Deborah Westcott

Janet Collins

Henry Josephson

Hannah Oram

Grace DiGiovanni

Ryan Chui Wai Yin

Christina Pero

Victoria Cobb

Eden-Lyn Thomas

Grace Styer

Chris Penman

David Cota-Buckhout

Kellie McCrea

Isabel Lopez-Molini

Joseph A Testani

Blaire Koerner

John Schloff

Roy Krishnan

Cathy Caiazza

Miriam Reesor

Eric Koester

Juliana Kilcoyne

Becca Martin

Madelyn Candela

Emily Andrews

Susan Sepkowski

Sydney Sisson

Evan Bushinsky

Kristin Smith

Remiah Sundine

Dana Damiani

Abby Gutowski

Daniel Reger

Rebecca O'Connor

Abigail Liebhart

Allan Sepkowski

Antonia Demopoulos

Cece Hylton

Caitlin Carrato

Jordana Cohen

Phoebe Konecky

Paola Rodriguez Tiel

Karen & Randy Wheeler

Colin P. Smith

Chloe Salone

Reena Caplash

Molly Fultz

Hannah O'Connor

Yang Wang

Colleen Mary Brereton

Katie Brereton

Erin Dietrick

Maya Haigis